Derwent Days

**Stories from the Derwent
and Hope Woodlands**

1998

Published by **Yorkshire Art Circus**, School Lane, Glasshoughton,
Castleford, West Yorkshire, WF10 4QH Tel: 01977 550401 Fax: 01977 512819
e-mail admin@artcircus.org.uk

Editing team: Jo Henderson, Sam Woods

Special thanks to Kathleen Birkinshaw and Michael Jolley

Production: Derwent Valley and Hope Woodlands Community, Gavin Bell, Lorna Hey,
Paul Miller

Photographs: From the Community, Emma Cocker, Peak National Park Archives

Cover design: Patrick Jackson

Printed by FM Repro, Roberttown, Liversedge.

ISBN: 1 898311 38 2

Classification: Social History

British Library Cataloguing in Publication Data.
A catalogue record for this book is available from the British Library.

Yorkshire Art Circus is a unique book publisher. We work to increase access to writing and
publishing and to develop new models of practice for arts in the community. Please write to us
for details of our full programme of workshops and our current book list.

Yorkshire Art Circus Web Site: www.artcircus.org.uk

Yorkshire Art Circus is supported by:

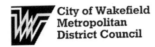

Contents

Contributors

Aiden Jones
Andrea Jolley
Andrew Skelton
Andy Shaw
Angela White
Barbara Morton
Betty Priestley
Bill Birkinshaw
Chris Oxley
Christine Woodhead
Clifford Morton
Colin Elliott
Dorothy Hitch
Emma Cocker
Emma Woods
Frank Booth
Gary Woodhead
Gavin Bell
Gavin Jones
Gill Jones
Graham Jones
Hannah Skelton
Harold Froggatt
Helen Woodhead
Joe Skelton
Joan Priestley
Joanne Woods
Joseph Rowarth

Judy Skelton
Julie Hutchinson
Kathleen Birkinshaw
Kiri Signora
Leonard Bridge
Mary Ayres
Mary Birkinshaw
Maurice Cottrill
Michael Jolley
Olive Booth
Penny Wright
Ray Colley
Ray Wallage
Rick Jones
Robert Jolley
Roger White
Ryan Jones
Sam Skelton
Samantha Woods
Simon Wright
Stan Hitch
Stephen Sampson
Tamsyn Wright
Tara White
Tom Jolley
Tristan Wright
William Eyre
William Woods

Ladybower Reservoir

Early morning in the Derwent Valley

Introduction

The Upper Derwent and Ashopton Valleys of the Peak National Park are among the wildest yet most visited areas of England. The reservoirs of the Upper Derwent receive almost two million visitors a year. Those that come to marvel at the wonders of the landscape and at the majesty of the dams may sometimes forget that the area is also the home and workplace to a diverse community of families and individuals, some whose families have lived and worked here for generations others relative newcomers. Some just chose to live here for sheer pleasure and others whose lives are inextricably linked to the land and caring for it - farmers, gamekeepers, foresters and employees of the Water Companies.

This book tells the tales of life past and present in this beautiful and dramatic area. Some of the stories are sad, some funny but above all help build a picture of what makes life special for those that live here.

The whole process of creating this book has been led by the community itself. Support and training with the writing, editing, design and publishing process was received from Yorkshire Art Circus. Two weekends of photography fun days (for children and adults alike) and training / advice on black and white photography were led by Emma Cocker of the Site Gallery, Sheffield.

All the stories and images present are written, produced and edited by the community. The Peak National Park Ranger Service and Severn Trent Water have provided assistance and support. Sponsorship was received from the National Lottery through the Arts Council of England, Rural Action, Severn Trent Water, Sheffield Photographic Centre and Jessops Photographic.

I hope you receive as much enjoyment reading this book as we have had making it.

Gavin Bell
Peak National Park Ranger
1998

Derwent and Hope Woodlands Women's Institute 1938

CHAPTER ONE
Looking Back

Joe Tagg was an old farmer who lived with his niece at Mill Cottage opposite the Derwent Post Office. When the valley was flooded in the nineteen forties, he was moved to the new village at Yorkshire Bridge, but he kept his tenancy for his few fields up Derwent above the new water line. Even though he was very old, he would walk up to them most days to do a little work, then have a little nap in his shed amongst the trees on his land before walking home. My father would fetch him into our farmhouse on cold days to warm him up, so he spent many hours in our kitchen. If one of us children were crying, he would slowly retrieve his cap from his pocket, carefully unfold it and hold it out to catch the tears.

He was accompanied in his latter years by his old bitch, Tip, and he often delighted us by delving into the 'Poachers' pocket of his coat and producing a couple of puppies that she was rearing at the time.

One day my mum was about to serve up a roast dinner in the kitchen when Joe arrived. She offered him some dinner, but he refused, saying that he had some sandwiches. She served the meal, popped into the cellar to fetch something and returned to find him sat down in her chair busily tucking into her dinner. All the food had been served so Mum gracefully kept quiet and had to go without her meal.

At shearing time Joe was in charge of the 'tar bucket'. This Stockholm tar was used to dress any shearing cuts, made accidentally by the shearers and kept flies off the wounds. When he went home, he often forgot that he was carrying the bucket and my sister Janet, was sent down the road to the big ash tree where he always got to before he realised he still had it and duly deposited it.

Joe was an excellent shepherd and was well known in the local sheepdog trials. He was so good that he once trained a labrador to work on sheep. It was he who taught me how to work sheep with a dog, on the steep land above Grainfoot Farm.

During World War II I remember once walking up Abbey Clough on Howden Moor with Joe, at the time there were practice ranges set up just over the hill at Broomhead Moor, where anti aircraft gunners would train. On this particular day an aeroplane was towing a huge windsock as a target for the gunners, shells seemed to be falling all around us, crashing and banging everywhere. He calmly turned to me and over the racket of the shells said, 'By 'eck lad, if one of them hits us it'll make a fair place for a scab!'

One day Joe's brother was travelling over the Snake Pass in a horse and trap, he dropped the reins at the top of the Pass and couldn't reach them. As the horse bolted down the hill, Mr Tagg climbed onto the shafts to try and retrieve them. He fell, was killed instantly and the horse never stopped until it reached the Oak Tree pub in Glossop.

I was sent from Foxhouse to Derwent in 1921, aged five, to live with my maternal grandparents at Grainfoot Farm. My two brothers were also sent there and we started school at Derwent in the spring term. We only went home to our parents about three times a year. It was a beautiful large farmhouse; the kitchen was nine yards square. There was a huge stone fireplace, which nearly covered one wall; there was a stove and a huge slate backstone for cooking oatcakes, then a set pot at the end for boiling the water for washing. Dozens of oatcakes were made on wash days when all the fires were stoked up. These were hung on a rack above the fireplace to dry. The last of the oatcake batter was spread thinly on the backstone and cooked until it curled up like brandy snaps. We call this 'Scrattle' I can still taste it now seventy years on. In front of the fire there was a screen-like contraption with loads of hooks on it. This was pushed up to the fire and bread or oatcakes were toasted on it.

From the big kitchen you went down four steps into the cellar, there were stone benches around the walls which harboured large flat pancheons of milk from which cream was skimmed each morning to make butter. We had a butter machine, which cut the butter into blocks and stamped it with a design. The

Grainfoot Farm

buttermilk was made into mouth-watering scones.

In the centre of the cellar was a stone salting bench. Every Christmas Grandfather killed four pigs for ham and bacon. This was a hard days work and everyone was roped in to help. I remember that my job was to sit on the salting bench on a folded hessian sack and shave the salt off the huge blocks with a carving knife. The salted sides of bacon were hung from the kitchen ceiling by large hooks.

The house was so big that it could be almost split in to two halves. It even had two staircases and a smaller kitchen at the far end of the house. Sometimes paying guests would rent half of the house for a while. One bedroom was so big that it had two four poster beds in it.

We had an indoor flush toilet at Grainfoot, almost unheard of on a farm. Outside there was a large earth closet with three seats in a row one of them being smaller for the children. There were squares of newspaper skewered on nails on the wall. The soil bins were emptied from the back of the closet. My uncle emptied the night soil. There were three pear trees and one cherry tree, which grew right up to the back of the house. My uncle would dig a trench around one of the trees and use the soil for compost filling the trench over with earth. You could pick the fruits from the back bedroom windows it was fantastic as pear juice exploded down your chin as you bit into one.

Grandfather had a Harley Davidson motorbike combination. He took the sidecar off as soon as he bought it and replaced it with a home made wooden box, which held up to seven sheep. Whenever there was a dog trial meeting the local men would get a lift with Grandfather; they would all stand in the box as Grandfather rode the bike in his long leather coat.

The last occupant of Grainfoot Cottage was Fred Wilson who worked for the Derwent Valley Water Board on the forestry section. He spent weeks planting trees then weeks felling and cutting trees. As he came home from work most nights he crossed the old disused railway line which had been used to transport stone to Derwent to build the reservoirs. He would saw off a section from an old railway sleeper, tuck it under his arm and take it home. That night he would

Lockerbrook Farm

chop the sleeper into firelighting sticks for use the following morning.

Joe Thorp lived at Riding House Farm near Grainfoot and the house had a pantry with a blue slate roof dug into the hillside behind the house. One day Mrs Thorp heard a tremendous crash from inside the pantry. She opened the door and found, to her astonishment, a horse standing there. It had walked onto the roof and fallen through. The only way to get the horse out was to lead it through the house and out of the front door. One can only imagine the tremendous clearing up task that followed.

Hill farming in a remote spot like Lockerbrook must always have been a subsistence occupation. I remember spending many holidays there as a boy and as a young man, for a decade or so during and after the Second World War.

A cousin of mine Harry Williams, who was several years my senior, was serving as an officer in the RAF and spending some days leave at Lockerbrook when a telegram arrived at his home in Studfield Road, Wisewood, recalling him to his squadron. There was no telephone at Lockerbrook and very few ordinary folk had a car in those days and the petrol ration was only available to essential users anyway, so I was despatched on my bike from our house in Lime Street.

The news could not have been carried from Aix to Ghent with more enthusiasm. This was a more exiting bit of war effort than collecting scrap iron with the boy scouts or turns at putting up the blackouts at the Sheffield Royal Infirmary. The route was through Malin Bridge, up the Rivelin Valley Road, over Moscar, past Ashopton Viaduct, (nearing completion) and along the Snake to Hagg Lane. All signposts had been removed hopefully to confuse invaders, so any travelling was a bit tricky. When I arrived waving the urgent piece cousin Harry hurriedly packed and set off on his bike. I stayed to become captivated by Lockerbrook and hence returned as often as I could.

Derwent Church and Village

The Wain family were old school, high church people. We all went to church twice on Sunday. Derwent Church had a full peal of bells, which had been donated by the Duke of Norfolk. In later years there was a stained glass window dedicated to my brother Edward after he was killed in a tragic accident. When the church was demolished in the nineteen forties the window was misplaced. After many years of searching for it I was told it was in the Derwent Valley Water Board Offices and went to find it. To my immense disappointment I found that it had been given to a troop of boy scouts who wanted the stained glass. The church demolition also meant that the Wain family graves were exhumed and re-buried in the churchyard at Grindleford under the shadows of some large Yew trees.

I attended Derwent public elementary school until I was ten years old. The headmistress was Miss Dixon and my teacher was Miss Hettie Bingham who was a family friend. It was only my second day at school when Miss Bingham, after countless warnings for talking in class, delivered serious punishment by smacking me hard on the wrist. I cried, not in pain, but with the shame and humiliation of being punished in front of the class. George and Hettie Bingham ran the Post Office at Derwent. They sold lemonade in cod bottles and you had to thump the marble to get the drink out. George was a bit slow with numbers and us kids would get all worked up, he used to shout 'Hettie, Hettie, they're here again, you'll have to come quick!'

The Catholic Schoolhouse had to close while I was at Derwent and about half a dozen children came to our school. The one concession was to allow them to go into a different room at prayer time so that they could recite their own prayers.

By the time the school closed Miss Bingham had been there some fifty years in total, the children would do anything for her, staying with her until they were eight years old. Young children would sit at the front and the older ones at the back. Miss Patten taught the juniors and was more severe, having a fifteen-inch cane, which she used regularly on anyone who stepped out of line. We all got sick of this so one day we took the cane outside and chopped it in half with

Derwent School Children 1933

a spade.

We had to get rid of the evidence, so I jumped over the wall into the churchyard and buried the pieces in a pile of earth. Miss Patten was livid, she questioned all of us, when it came to my turn I couldn't lie, I had to go back outside and dig up the pieces. I was smiling all over my face when I gave them back to her, as I knew she couldn't cane me.

The schoolhouse was let to a family. We never dared to go near there, as they weren't on good terms with us. Footballs or cricket balls were always breaking the windows. The man of the house was in the army and struck terror in us when he was home on leave, He would fly over the wall into the schoolyard at the slightest provocation and really box ears or thump us.

The only water at school was in a trough in the schoolyard. You drank from it and even washed your hands in it when necessary. Everyone respected the trough, as it was the only water there.

At dinner time all us kids would play in the village with it only being a few houses. Tiggy was the favourite game and every one of us used to play. One day there were thirty-two of us playing a game that I had started, and somehow all but three of us ended up down a coal cellar in one of the houses. When the whistle for lessons was blown, the last three shut the cellar door and put a stone flag over it and went into school. We sat for twenty minutes in front of a bemused teacher, denying all knowledge of where the other children were. We were sent out to find them, and had to open the cellar doors and let them all out.

There was a beautiful pear tree in the garden at Wellhead Farm just up from the school. This was a constant temptation to all of us kids. The farmer, Harold Bradbury, used to hear us coming up the hill from school and let this enormous evil looking dog out into the garden. He would set it over the wall at us, barking and chasing up and down; we would scatter in all directions. It was years later that I found out that the dog was as soft as a brush and that Harold only did it for the fun of it.

Local families along the Hope Woodlands Valley used to take it in turns to hold the Sunday prayer meetings in their houses. Well the families thought that we should have a place to worship so we asked the then landowner, The Duke of Devonshire, if he would build us a chapel. He would not do this but he did give us the ground at Gillot on which we could build our own. I don't know where the money came from but the chapel was built and I can remember going to Sunday school and getting a certificate of attendance.

There were only six children at the Sunday school and I was the only boy. Whenever we did plays or anything like that, I always had to be in them. The teacher would fetch me from home if I didn't turn up. Once we were reading the Bible aloud in the chapel, doing one paragraph each, I could not read that well and my bit had lots of long words in it. When it came to my turn I said to the teacher, 'I'll just listen!' It was the only time that the teacher had known me to stop talking.

We were each given a penny to put in the collection box after Sunday school. We would each take a ha'penny of our own and put that in instead - keeping the penny and thereby making a ha'penny for ourselves.

When the Methodist Chapel was built at Ashopton, Mr Jonathon Cotterill - the publican at the Ladybower Inn made a generous offer to donate lighting in the form of oil lamps. The trustees declined this offer as they thought it would be improper to accept a gift from a man who made his living from the sale of alcohol. A short time later however they returned cap in hand to say that perhaps they would like some oil lamps after all. Obviously this was preferable to worshipping in the dark.

Life up Derwent was very community based and quiet by town standards. We were never bored and spent nights sewing, knitting and crocheting. The summer fruit was preserved in bottles, eggs were pickled, vegetables salted. We always had a huge vegetable garden to maintain. Community whist drives were held at Derwent School and afterwards there would be a dance. Mrs Downing would play the piano and her husband would accompany her on the cello. In later years a trio from Moscar would play the dance music, having a drummer to keep time. There were special whist drives at Christmas and New Year; the hall would be decorated with a beautiful evergreen garland that went all round the room. There were prizes of pheasants and hares for the various games.

We rarely went out of the valley. Meat and groceries were delivered weekly from Bamford, Hope or Hathersage. Trips to Sheffield were only for special provisions or clothes. No buses came up the valley, but you could sometimes get a lift on Marsdens milk wagon, sitting on the churns with only makeshift cushions for comfort. Aunt Blanche however would ride to Sheffield on her bike laden with homemade butter and eggs to sell. She would have panniers on the back and bags hanging on the handlebars. Mum always said that Blanche was killed by hard work.

'I moved from Sheffield to Derwent in 1929 when I married David Priestley of Jubilee Cottages, I immediately fell in love with the valley and its changing seasons, so did many rambling and cycling clubs, why not cater for them I thought. David made me a sign saying Pot of tea and hot water 4d, Ham and eggs 2/6d, Special offer brown bread and butter, marmalade and jam, a scone and pot of tea for the princely sum of 1/3d. Bed and breakfast was my next venture at 3/6d a night.

Joan my youngest sister came for a short stay age 13 months and never went home.

Age four, I started attending Derwent C of E School, every Monday proudly taking 1/1d for two 6d saving stamps and 1d for a cup of cocoa each school day. Each summer we looked forward to a trip to the coast, treated by the church and at Christmas time we were invited to a party in Derwent Hall.

What great fun we children had riding through the newly constructed pipebridge on an hastily made go cart. Wintertime often found me in the company of Harry Shirt and Joe Bowden in the sawmill at Fairholmes, the mill used coal and was one of the warmest places around.'

In 1955 Joan married Alan Priestly (no relation to David) and continued to live with Bet and David till 1958.

Olive Ollerenshaw was born in 1910 at Dingbank Farm, Ashopton.

'With three sisters and four brothers we enjoyed playing ball games and hide and seek in summer. I remember the very cold winters, we often sat in the parlour and sang hymns accompanied by Father on the organ. Dingbank had a Yorkshire range which had to be black leaded every Saturday come rain, hail or shine!

Around 1933 Frank Booth a farmlad for Tom Wain at Grainfoot Farm started courting me. We married in 1938 on December 22nd in Ashopton Methodist Chapel. A cold, cold day with snow on the ground, I wore a beautiful red velvet dress, made by myself. My only bridesmaid was my youngest sister Frances. It was to be the last wedding in the Chapel before most of Ashopton village was demolished.

We continued to live at Dingbank, Frank working for Derwent Water Board at the sawmill and helping to plant Win Hill.

At the bottom of Wood Lane, Ashopton was a field called Fringewell Bottom, where in summertime scouts from Lancashire camped. Every Friday they gave a concert and all the locals were invited to attend. Every fortnight we attended the whist drive and dance in Derwent.

My Uncle Tom lived in the cottage above Grainfoot Farm. His wife was a lovely singer. On Sunday nights she would often sing for us as we sat around the piano. We three boys were all taught piano by a Miss Annie Cotterill who lived at Ginnet House. My Auntie Annie Wain would make me practice at home. As I struggled with my playing she would often shout from the other room, 'Joseph, I don't think that note was quite right, try it again'.

There was a long wood behind the cart shed which ran most of the way to Ashopton. We would gather sack loads of hazelnuts from the trees there and they stayed good all winter. Alongside this wood ran the Long Meadow and we were enlisted by Uncle Tom to turn the swathes by hand, using rakes. There was a horse-drawn swathe turner in the farm yard and the horses were stood idle in the stable, but we had to do it all by hand.

At Old House Farm, we were the first in the valley to have a television - a huge box of a thing with a tiny screen. When it was the Queen's Coronation, all the locals were invited for a party and to watch the event on television. The front room was filled with rows of chairs and we all strained to see what was happening on the fuzzy black and white screen. Our electricity came from a generator and the picture would jump and flicker wildly unless you put all the lights on in the house to make the generator work more evenly. A similar crowd also turned up on FA Cup Final days. We always put Alf Hammond, the gamekeeper at the front, as his antics were often more entertaining than the football match itself.

During the war the wireless was an important feature in every home. Listening to the nine o'clock news was an almost sacramental ritual. In the depths of a Lockerbrook winter, it was the only link with the outside world. Comedians like Sir Harry Lauder, Will Hay and Tommy Handley and singers like Gracie Fields were amongst some of the favourites. As there was no electricity the set worked off devices known as 'accumulators' a kind of battery contained in a big, heavy glass jar with zinc plates and some sort of solution inside. A pair of these had to be taken to Bamford once a month for recharging.

Bachelors Tea, Ashopton

Every year Derwent and Woodlands Shepherds Society held their meeting at the Snake Inn. Pens were set aside for farmers to put any unidentified sheep in. The assembled members would identify their sheep- there being released after a payment of fee. Any unclaimed animals were auctioned off - the money raised being used to buy the shepherds a good dinner and their first drink at the Snake immediately after the sale. These dinners were often the highlight of the year, each shepherd paying a shilling a year subscription, this also going towards payment for the meal. After the meal there was much drinking and a good singsong.

Another annual event was organised by the young men of Derwent and Ashopton. They would collect donations of food from all the local houses and gather together for the Bachelors Tea, this would take place at Ashopton Chapel where a lovely meal would be provided for the local people, while the young men 'waited on'. Afterwards when the tables had been cleared, the chairs were arranged to face a makeshift stage where the young men would entertain their guests by dressing as different characters and perform dialogues.

Derwent and Woodlands Women's Institute was formed in 1934 and had monthly meetings in Derwent Hall. Speakers covered various subjects; rugcraft, stoolseating and dressmaking, were amongst the many. Raffles were held every meeting costing a halfpenny a ticket. At one meeting the grand total of one shilling and two pence was made.

Meetings were suspended in 1940; minutes of December 1939 read,

'Owing to the outbreak of war and subsequent traffic regulations, this meeting wonders if it is possible to continue during the blackout and bleak winter months.'

The final meeting was April 6 1940, the minutes read,

'Derwent and Woodlands wish to state the happiness and aid the W.I. has brought to all members and that no institute can have closed with greater regret.'

The members promised to reform again as soon as possible. It was reformed twenty years later on February 4 1960 and is still going strong. Meetings are held monthly in St. Henry's school room, Derwent. Some of our members' mothers attended the original W.I. Subjects covered these days include first aid, keep fit and dough modelling. Activities are high on today's agenda with ten-pin bowling, evening walks and cream teas.

Derwent's vicar was Mr Rowse; he was a lovely vicar. He always visited us on Thursdays as this was mother's baking day and he always said that he loved the smell of baking bread. She baked all day long. White bread, brown bread, teacakes and 'cut and come again' cake with currants.

He had special permission from the Duke of Norfolk to fish the river Derwent and shoot on the surrounding land. Many of the local farmers supplied Mr Rowse with cartridges so that he would shoot rabbits on their ground. On a Friday afternoon during the season he could always be found, standing in the river with waders on pulling out trout. He was once shooting rabbits with the local gamekeeper, Hugh Ellis. The men argued over a dead rabbit, both claiming it as their own. 'Tha weren't even shootin' int' same field' said Mr Ellis. Mr Rowse then questioned the gamekeeper's prowess as a shooter. 'Right' said the disgruntled gamekeeper, 'Thee throw thas 'at int' air an' I show thee what a shot I am.' The vicar not to be bluffed at immediately did so, where upon the gamekeeper raised his gun and blew a big hole in the hat before it hit the floor.

Mr Rowse once caught a young boy, Jess Thorpe, up a pear tree. 'Come down from that tree Jess.' Said Mr Rowse in his posh voice.

'I'm not coming down while tha's there!' replied Jess, as he knew that he'd get his ears boxed.

Jess Eyre once rode his bike from Derwent into Hope village. As he came to dismount outside a shop, he fell off his bike and landed in a crumpled heap.

'Ee, are you hurt?' asked a lady passer by.
'No.' said Jess; 'I always get off this way!'

Miss Annie Cotterill did the deliveries for Percy Law, the butcher in the nineteen forties. One day she dropped a sheep's head off at a Derwent house. This was an obviously cheap cut of meat at that time and as she drove off to the next delivery, she realised that she had taken the meat to the wrong address. She quickly turned around and went back to retrieve the meat, but on returning to the house found that the wrongful recipients already had the sheep's head in a pan on the stove, coming to the boil. The family couldn't even afford a sheep's head and were not about to let this windfall slip through their hands.

Annie Cotterill lived alone at Ginett House, Ashopton, since the death of her mother in 1939, remaining there until her death in 1989, only months before her hundredth birthday. The house had no electricity; the plumbing consisted only of a flush toilet upstairs and a single cold tap into a large pot in the kitchen sink. She refused to drink this water and instead fetched her drinking water in a bucket from a stone trough in the back yard.

As she grew older she did make one concession by allowing the social services to install a telephone at Ginett, for her to use in an emergency. As the telephone was somewhat modern in appearance and therefore unsightly Miss Cotterill hid it under a specially knitted telephone cosy.

Her independence never ceased to amaze me and she retained her incredible memory throughout her life. No visit to her house was ever brief, and we would sit for hours in the spotless kitchen with its stone flagged floor, rag rugs and beautiful black leaded range which she never lit under any circumstances. 'Oh no dear.' She would say, 'It uses a bucket full of coal, makes an awful lot of dust and takes ages to clean.'

We always sat around a huge kitchen table in the centre of the room, over which hung the only source of light - a paraffin lamp, while the paraffin cooker would glug and smoke gently in the background, permanently lit in winter for

The Cotterill Family at Ginett House

warmth as well as cooking. Mice could often be heard or glimpsed scurrying around in the shadows at the room edges, much to my mother's horror. 'It won't stay dear,' she reassured Mum, 'I don't drop any crumbs so there's nothing for it to live on in here.'

Once when my father was visiting, a bewildered looking mole sauntered in under the back door. 'Take it outside and let it go.' She said unperturbed.

Her stories of her colourful lifetime were endless, and gave a rare glimpse into a century of experiences both happy and sad, from her childhood years in America, where she was born, through the early nineteen hundreds when her family moved back to Ashopton and the Ladybower Inn which was owned by her grandparents.

In the First World War she became a nurse in Nottingham and later an accomplished pianist, giving lessons to young pupils and playing herself at dances after whist drives at Bamford, Hathersage and Derwent, after which she would cycle home alone in the early hours of the morning.

She remembered the day when an enormous traction engine was brought up through the Ashopton and Derwent villages to be used for the construction of the Derwent and Howden dam walls. The whole village turned out to see this monstrous machine, and stared in wonder as the engineers worked to get enough steam up to get the machine up the steep winding 'vicarage hill' at Derwent. The engine only managed a short distance before losing steam, its wheels having to be blocked again and again until another head of steam had built up.

She saw the valley she loved ruined by the upheaval of all the local families, the destruction of the beautiful farms and houses, and the sad loss of Derwent Hall and Church, also the Ashopton Chapel. When the valley finally flooded almost up to her front door step, one of the grandest views in the area had been lost - a loss which she grieved for the rest of her life.

As Miss Cotterill grew older she established firm opinions on various subjects and once formed, they were unchangeable. On seeing the RAF camouflage planes flying down the valley, she said that they were 'Old patched up ones', given to the trainee pilots to practice in.

She eventually took to wearing a heavy wool coat in the house during winter, as she moved so slowly and felt the cold so much. As she shuffled along one day, she caught sight of her reflection in the mirror and there on her shoulder was a small bird half-asleep. It must have come through an open window, as they were always open at her insistence, whatever the weather, to give plenty of fresh air. She walked to the back door and stood there for a while until the bird flew away.

Gathering Sheep at Slippery Stones

CHAPTER TWO
Snow, Coal and Sheep

The winter of nineteen forty seven was the worst one we ever had at Derwent. I had gone into partnership with my brother-in-law, and both our families lived at Old House Farm, Derwent. It started to snow in January, and more and more fell each day with driving winds and very low temperatures. At first we weren't too concerned as we had plenty of food and coal for the house. The barn was full of hay too. Some neighbours came on almost immediately to borrow buckets of coal, and we even ended up sending food on for them sometime later. When the weather showed no sign of letting up we started to get worried.

In the first weeks the Derwent Valley Water Board sent a gang of men on digging out the Derwent road, but the snow blew in behind them as fast as they could dig, so the idea was abandoned. We only had a horse-drawn snow plough which proved useless in these conditions.

Plans were made to get grocery supplies up the valley using a boat on the reservoir which was successful until the reservoir froze over as temperatures plummeted. Luckily the telephones kept on working. This was amazing because the overhead lines were thick with ice and almost touching the ground. One line did snap and we repaired it ourselves and it worked perfectly.

As supplies dwindled we rang Howes, the grocers at Bamford and asked them to send someone up with our food order plus several other people's orders to Ashopton. I set off with the horse laden with panniers down the east side of the valley to meet him. The road was treacherous. One section had a steep bank straight from the roadside to the reservoir. There was so much drifted snow that I couldn't see where the track was. I almost turned back as it was so dangerous, but ended up dismounting and leading the horse gently along as I felt for the track. We managed to get through though it took a long time.

Sam Bingham was waiting for me at the end of the road and remarked then, and many times since, that I looked just like a snowman on a horse, emerging from the wilderness.

We soon ran out of hay for the cattle, and arranged to buy some from Crookhill Farm across the valley. We rigged up an old curved piece of corrugated iron sheet from an Anderson shelter and put it behind the horse to act as a large sledge. It worked well to cart the hay on.

The sheep were all out on the moors so we spent many days trying to get to them. It was pitiful to see the backs of the walls that edged onto the moors, as they were full of dead sheep, up to seven deep in places. The weather would drive the sheep down for shelter until they could go no further and were trapped under the walls - the bottom sheep all being smothered - the top sheep surviving if they were lucky. In places there were snowdrifts up to sixty feet high. There was no bare ground on Howden, but over the hill on Strines and Broomhead moors there was relatively little snow. The wind had gradually blown all the snow across into our valley.

The sheepdogs found one sheep buried in a drift which had been stuck for at least a month. We dug it out and couldn't believe it when it ran off like a march hare up the moor. We managed to get some young ewes off the moor and put them into Joe Tagg's field which was the only field around that had some bare ground on it where the wind had swept it. They soon died because they were so weak and we had no hay for them. There were dead rabbits, hares and birds everywhere - all just starved to death. Any sheep that did survive miscarried due to the stress - and were like walking skeletons.

The children were excited at first by the amount of snow, but they soon tired of it, and everybody had to fight depression as things got worse.

When the thaw finally came we moved cart loads of dead sheep. We lost eighty percent of our flock. Later that spring we noticed that bark was missing from the top branches of some very tall sycamores in Walker Clough. It had been eaten by rabbits, as these were the only parts of the trees showing from the snow drifts.

One snowy winter's day, when the Derwent and Howden reservoirs were being built, a navvy from the works decided, against local advice, to walk over Cutgate track to Langsett where the Langsett Reservoir was also being built.

Rescuing Sheep in Buried Snow

He never arrived, and his body was not found until the following August, crouched behind a rock where he had frozen to death.

Before the construction of the railway to nearby Bamford the local farmers, to get coal from the Derwent, would get up at 3.00 a.m. and set off in convoy, each with a horse and cart plus a 'chain horse' tied behind to help pull the load up the steeper hills. They would travel to 'Sheard's Pit' at Dronfield, and when loaded with coal would start the long haul home.

The first part of the journey, to the top of Holmesfield, was most arduous, being uphill all the way, and the 'chain horse' was essential. The convoy stopped at the Robin Hood Inn, Holmesfield, where the horses were fed, watered and rested while the men went inside for a meal. Spirits were often high as this was one of the rare occasions that the men left the valley, especially in such a large group. From Holmesfield the journey was much easier, and the men would be home by the evening. In the summer, when coal sales were slow, the pit would transport the coal to the Fox House Inn Longshaw, where it was collected by the farmers.

I delivered coal up Derwent for many years. When delivering coal to Ashes and High House farms, we could only get about half way up the track. The coal was tipped at the side of the track and we backed the lorry down. Mr Ollerenshaw at The Ashes would cart his coal the rest of the way with a horse and mulch cart. Willie Elliott, further up the lane at High House would bring his petrol driven Allen Soythe, a grass mowing machine with metal wheels driven also by the engine. He had a little trailer fixed behind it, and shovelled coal into it, then walked up the lane driving his odd contraption up home many times to get all his coal home.

When Mr Mathy Ollerenshaw moved from Ashes Farm to St. Henrys, a cottage in Derwent itself, I was asked to bring my coal lorry to help with

Ashes Farm

the move. Mr Ollerenshaw lived with his wife, Winnie and her sister Liza. It was snowing on the day, and my lorry was slipping on the cobbled yard. If Mr Ollerenshaw had one box of ashes, he had thirty, and used these to help the lorry get a grip on the stones. The kitchen was full of boxes, and as I loaded these up, more appeared. By the time the lorry was full the kitchen was still full of boxes. I couldn't get up for a second load, so Mr Ollerenshaw had to use his horse and cart a few days later to finish the job, once the snow had gone.

In the early nineteen thirties, when I was a teenager, I lived on my father's farm at Hathersage, my work being split between the farm and the family coal business. Each Friday tea-time I would have to take the coal lorry to Hathersage where I collected dozens of grocery orders for the houses of Derwent and Ashopton. These had to be delivered that night, and as some of the houses were off the beaten track I had to do a lot of walking. It was often nearing midnight when I arrived at Lanehead farm, high above Derwent village, and sometimes had to wake the family to give them their order.

In 1933 I began working for my father at Brough Corn Mill. One day father called me to his office and told me that I would have to do the Derwent and Woodlands round, as my cousin who normally did the job was ill. I told him that I'd never driven a car before on the load, but he just said 'You will learn as you go'.

Shortly I found myself smartened up, with all the relevant paperwork, in my cousin's car struggling up the Derwent road. I muddled through the morning's work, then spent my dinner hour driving up past Grainfoot Farm, through Derwent Village and up the steep hill to Wellhead, then going back again until I had mastered double-de-clutching and getting the engine's revs right for good gear changing.

I eventually travelled to Derwent and Woodlands on a more regular basis and got to know the locals quite well. Grainfoot Farm, which was farmed by the Wain family was a favourite call - the house had the biggest kitchen I've ever seen - having several tables and large dressers.

Mr Swallows, at Lanehead was a character - always waiting for me with his hat and coat on. I had to take him to the Ladybower Inn and buy him a few drinks before he would pay me his standing account and place another order. The minimal profit we made from his custom would never have covered the drinking expenses he incurred.

Delivering chicken feed to Mrs Parkinson up at the Abbey was always a long job, not because of the size of the order, but because of her ability to talk. I don't think that she had many visitors so she made the most of it when we called there. Many of the farms were difficult to get to with our old lorries. We once struggled up to the Ashes Farm with a load of corn for Mathy Ollerenshaw, and were very relieved to have finally made it up the steep lane into his yard.

'Where's my corn?' asked Mathy, looking puzzled.

'It's on the back.' I replied.

'No it isn't,' he said.

We had lost all the sacks on the way up the steep gravel lane, so we had to go back and pick them all up. Luckily in those days the sacks were hessian so none of them burst. On another occasion we were delivering to Two Thorn Fields farm up Derwent Woodlands, when it began to snow heavily. We put snow chains on the wheels and carried on. As we came back down the farm lane, empty and in bottom gear, I realised that the brakes on the lorry were not working. The lorry picked speed up and shot down the lane out of control and straight onto the Snake Road which, fortunately for us was clear of traffic. When we finally stopped we found that one of the snow chains had broken and slashed through a brake pipe.

Bill Simpson was once delivering Albert Shepherd's order of 16 stone bags of corn to Bridge End Farm. He would have to park the lorry on the roadside and unload the bags onto the parapet of the old packhorse bridge.

Once the lorry was empty he would pick the bags up again and carry them across the bridge to the farm and into the barn. One day a bag slipped off the wall of the bridge and landed, unharmed, on a large boulder in the river. Bill merely scrambled down the steep bank, knelt down in the river, retrieved the bag and climbed back up the bank. Many people insisted that he was the strongest man in Hope Valley.

In 1919 my parents decided to move from Lockerbrook to another farm on the Woodhead Pass near Haslett Station. My dad told me that although we really loved Lockerbrook and it held a special place in our hearts, we had to look on the practical side of things. Transport was always a problem and you had to travel long distances for even the most essential items. So when I was four we moved.

About a week before the traction engine from Pickfords was due to come we started carrying our furniture and belongings down to Rowlee Farm. My father had let stock run down as much as possible and the first thing he had to do was walk the 80 or so sheep over to Cut Gate and left them at a farm there. This took him two days as I remember and the people at the farm were kind enough to put Dad up for the night. On the day, we were to move the traction engine arrived, friends helped to load up and the engine was off. The route for our furniture was up over the Snake Pass and out towards the Woodhead Pass. On the way up the Snake, the gubbins on the engine burnt out and the engine driver had to let the fire go out. He had to walk to the Station at Woodhead and catch a train into Sheffield and bring out a replacement part the next day. He fixed the engine, built a fire and arrived at Ranah Farm, our new home late that day.

In the meantime, Mum and me had walked to Hope station and caught the train to Sheffield. We then caught a train out to Haslett Station and arrived the same afternoon expecting to see the traction arriving about the same time. Dad left the same day as us and had to walk the eight or nine cattle by road

Ashopton Village

over Strines to our new place. My brother and sister followed him on the horse and cart with the poultry. Anyway, we were at our new home but had no idea what had happened to our furntiture. I was excited about my new bed. There was a large cupboard, the door of which swung up and was hooked onto a ceiling beam. A large wire sprung bed dropped down and as we had no bedding my mother made up a bed with our coats.

My father, a veterinary surgeon, was based at Hillsborough and attended many of the farms in Derwent and Ashopton. He used to make a lineament for rubbing on horses legs for sprained tendons and other ailments. This foul-smelling concoction was also in great demand among the farmers themselves to cure their own rheumatism.

One of the main ingredients for this lineament was egg and every year we would make the trip to Bridge End Farm at Derwent to collect our supply. My mother would pickle these, raw, in big stoneware jars to last throughout the winter months when, in those days, the hens had stopped laying.

I can vividly remember my first trip to Derwent with my mother and father in about 1912 in their pony and trap. We drove up the valley and arrived outside Derwent Hall at the end of the packhorse bridge. Bridge End Farm was across the river and rather than using the ford lower downstream, Mr Albert Shepherd, the farmer, came out to us and released the pony from its shafts, leaving the trap on the roadside. He led the pony across the bridge to be fed and stabled while we had tea with the Shepherd family before returning home that night with our eggs

Doctor Shepherd was the local G.P. who lived at Castleton. He received a message by word of mouth that somebody was very ill at Alport Valley. After finishing surgery and local rounds, the doctor rode over Hope Brinks on his horse, up and down the Snake Valley and up to Alport. It was late by the time the doctor arrived, and the house was in darkness.

The doctor knocked at the door for a while until one of the bedroom windows slid open and a man's head popped out. 'Who's ill?' said Dr Shephard. 'It's me, doctor,' he replied, 'I've got a sore throat. What will I do?

'Cut the bleeder!' said the Doctor through gritted teeth as he turned his horse and rode off back down the lane.

When my grandad was about four years old, and Aunt came to visit from Stockport, Grandad pestered his parents all day to be allowed to go home with her for a few days. They reluctantly agreed, and he went back to Stockport. As night fell, however, Grandad became upset and would not settle. In desperation his Aunt dressed him, took him to the railway station and caught the train to Hathersage. There followed a very long walk from the village to the outlying farmstead where he lived. In the early hours of the morning they reached the farm driveway, whereupon Grandad turned to his hapless Aunt and said 'It's alright, I can manage from here'.

Hayridge Farm, where I live now, was originally built as a corn mill by a man named Mr Shaw. The farm is made with large river washed stones with a rubble middle - hardly any stones go right through the walls. Mr Shaw was going to take water from the river Alport, and had a tunnel built, both ends started at the same time to speed the job up. The tunnels never met, however, and the mill was never finished. Subsequent investigation by the Derwent Valley Water Board found that the tunnels only missed each other by 4 feet. Another tunnel was built at the turn of the century to take water from the river Alport through the hill to Derwent Reservoir. My mother and her brother used to cycle through the tunnel into Derwent Valley to go to whist drives and dances, as it saved miles, and you didn't get wet if it rained.

Grandad used to farm Bank Top farm up Westend. His sister would ride the old 'salt track' from Westend to Glossop to go shopping. She was able to knit a pair of socks while riding the horse - one sock on the way to Glossop, the other on the way back.

When the famous *Dambusters* film was being made at Derwent, we saw it as a way to get ourselves immortalised on film. Every time the aeroplane, a camera fixed underneath, flew down the valley, the local women and children would run outside into their gardens and wave frantically at the camera. The poor director must have despaired as yards of his film ended on the cutting room floor, trying to find a suitable shot of the valley without the unwanted 'film stars'. If you watch the film it always cuts out before the ground shots reach our houses.

Willy Elliott lived at High House Farm above Derwent village until the early nineteen seventies, by which time he was in his nineties. Locals used to joke that the reason he lived so long was because he had plenty of older sisters to carry him about as a child, and hardly walked anywhere himself until he was about five years old.

When his wife, Blanche, was alive she would walk over the hill to 'Cut-throat Bridge', Moscar, where she caught the bus to Sheffield. Her return journey was always the same route, only loaded with heavy shopping. She said that this was easier than catching a bus to the village of Derwent and walking the steep path directly up to the farm.

I remember one 'shearing day' at High House. We hand sheared the sheep all morning and laid the fleeces in a pile at the side of the shed. At lunchtime we all filed into the house to find the meal set out for us, but there was no sign of Mrs Elliott. After lunch we returned to the shed to find all the fleeces had been neatly wrapped in our absence by Mrs Elliott, of

Lancaster Bomber flying over the valley

whom there was still no sign. She obviously preferred to work behind the scenes.

Sheep shearing always took place from mid June and through July. We sheared by hand, and travelled from farm to farm in a type of rota. Each farm had a specific day on which it sheared - our day at Hayridge Farm was the twenty first of June. If you had to miss a day because of bad weather, you had to go to the end of the list as it were. This often meant that farmers sheared their sheep damp, rather than lose their 'day'. The local gamekeepers always helped at shearing time, catching sheep for the shearers and wrapping fleeces. There was a lot of etiquette in the shearing shed. The best shearers were always put nearest to the door - the slowest at the back of the shed. The catchers never left the poorest sheep until last before dinner as these took longest to shear. My father was very skilled at sharpening hand shears, and often didn't get clipping himself until dinner time due to sharpening two pairs of shears per shearer.

Dinner time on shearing days were tremendous. Shearers often brought their wives along to help in the kitchens and serve the large joints of mutton, accompanied by huge basins full of mint sauce. This was followed by puddings and mugs of tea. One day Eric Elliott came in after a morning's clipping and sat to the table. After eating his dinner he ordered mug after mug of tea. The women were perplexed as Eric had about twenty or so mugs of tea, and the women made pot after pot for him. To the end of the meal nobody could hold their laughter any more, and Eric let the women into his ruse by producing a bucketful of tea from under the table.

Up until the nineteen forties there was a premium paid for wool which had been washed previous to shearing. This was done by gathering the sheep to specially built pens by a river. Men threw the sheep into a pool where oilskin clad colleagues rubbed and did their best to remove dirt and natural oils from the fleece.

The Howden Wash, Washing Sheep

It was agreed that the shepherds who gathered the sheep off the moors should not go into the river, as the combination of sweating with the walking while gathering, and the coldness of the river water would be hazardous to health. One farmer from the woodlands once did both jobs, and was dead within three days from pneumonia.

The Gee family at Rowlee farm were the last to use the sheep wash at Woodlands. I used to push the sheep under with a large pole instead of going in the wash. One day I fell in, and clung to a large sheep which swam out with me.

One of the Shepherd family who lived at Gillott Hey Farm spent the last seven years of his life in bed. Every so often, other members of the family would bring lambs into his bedroom at various stages of growth for him to look at and inspect.

I hadn't been left school long when I was asked to help with the sheep gathering at Mossy Lea farm on the Snake Road. There were three of us young lads went on the gather, and when we returned we all went in for dinner.

Mr Shepherd, the farmer would treat everybody as if they were a young lad - even his grown-up sons.

'What have you seen then?' he brusquely asked me.

'Nothing much', I replied innocently, 'but I've had to leave a ewe and two lambs by that dead cow.' There was total silence for what seemed like an eternity, then the whole kitchen suddenly erupted into fury, as father and sons clashed. 'I knew we had one missing' shouted one. 'We turned twenty-one cows up there last spring and only twenty came back in!' As the three men argued furiously and blamed all and sundry, us boys quietly left the room. I don't think that I ever said anything again as innocently as that and got such a response.

I remember Joe Tagg telling me about the rabbit drives that Mr T K Wilson, the shooting tenant, organised at Derwent. Rabbits were captured in box traps which consisted of a stone lined pit at the entrance to rabbit runs through stone walls. The pit was covered with a wooden lid which had a spring trap door in its centre. Normally rabbits ran over the lid, but when set, the door could catch huge numbers of rabbits at one time.

The rabbits were transported to a secure shed where they were housed and fed until the day of the rabbit shoot. Then they were loaded into baskets and released into a well-walled filed for the 'guns' to shoot at. This shoot traditionally took place on Boxing Day, and Old House Farm, Derwent, has a field called the 'Boxing Day piece' because of this.

In 1923, when I was fifteen, walking up the Foulstone track to meet Willy Elliott of High House Farm at Derwent, to go grouse beating. We did the 'Long Drag' drive that day on Howden Moors, and the daily pay rate was ten shillings, which, at that time, was an awful lot of money, especially for a schoolboy.

Mr T K Wilson had the grouse shooting on Howden Moor and was an avid sportsman, employing a total of seventeen gamekeepers as far away as Lincolnshire. At the end the shooters 'retired' to the 'Shooting Lodge' at Derwent for tea and refreshments made by the gamekeeper's wife.

At home

CHAPTER THREE
Living Here Now

My home is special to me because if I didn't have a home I would always be cold, hungry and maybe even have to beg. I feel sorry for people who don't have homes. I always wish I could help them in some way. I like living in Derwent and not in a town because in a town you can't just go out the front door and have a short stroll round the fields and meadows. When you open your door in the town the first noise you hear is 'NEEOWWW' (cars roaring past). But when you open the door in the countryside you hear birds singing - the trees whistling. My favourite part of the day in the countryside is the evening.

As National Trust Wardens, we are expected to live as near as possible to our own patch. This means that we can build up relationships with the local people and the tenant farmers.

As a representative of the landowner, my job is to work with the farm tenants, gamekeepers and the public.

My work is varied, with my dog Mac I help gather sheep with the farmers, I help gamekeepers with heather burning to maintain the moors, protect the environment, help to put out accidental moorland fires and promote the National Trust.

We have areas on Bleaklow, which are being destroyed by the effects of acid rain. The rain kills off the fragile plant life and the peat soil is washed away.

We are in the Environmentally Sensitive Areas scheme. Some areas of moorland are fenced off to keep the sheep from grazing and encourage regeneration. We take fixed point photographs of the area to monitor vegetation change over a period of 20 to 30 years.

I also manage some woodland, none of which is commercially viable. We plant new trees to ensure the continuation of the woodland.

Each moor is split and farmers have grazing licences, each area being allowed a certain number of sheep.

I like living in the Valley, working my dogs and working with the farmers. Sometimes it is difficult when members of the public park in our lane blocking us in without realising it. During the dry months, the risk of fire also causes problems. We need to educate the public more about the damage caused to the environment by moorland fires, as I am sure no one would start a fire on purpose.

There was once a fire on Bleaklow and Simon Booth loved driving our machines Garron and Octad (eight wheel drive jobs used to fight fires). On this particular day Tank Commander Simon raced out to be the first into the Garron, driving around doing scary manoeuvres. Once the fire was out and we all had finished, everyone headed back to Doctors Gate to get in to the pub. Tank Commander Simon drove back to Doctors Gate and on the way the machine he was driving shed a track. We were all into the pub enjoying a few pints of beer and poor Simon was left waiting for someone to come to his aid.

Using what most visitors regard as the 'traffic free road' from Fairholmes to Derwent, produces some very interesting reactions when people see a family in an ordinary car passing them. Scowls, stares and obvious spoken comments are common place and we often try and guess what people are saying, but as yet we have not had an experience like that of another resident who had a cyclist throw his bike down in front of a car.

Once when driving to the top end of the valley in my works Land Rover I was stopped by a walker who told me I should be walking like everyone else. Somewhat dumbfounded, I explained (very diplomatically) that I needed a vehicle to transport tools and materials and to enable efficient use of my time where long distances and steep gradients were involved. He was not listening, so I acknowledged his view and drove away. In retrospect I should have told him that if he was ever in trouble miles from the nearest surfaced road, I would walk to his aid.

Sheep Dipping

A few years ago there was an incident reported of a man in his sixties falling off his bike after a suspected heart attack, luckily it was angina. I went up with some part time rangers to the 'incident area' to assist until the ambulance arrived. We made sure that he was comfortable and monitored his condition. He was calm and coherent.

'I am sorry for causing you chaps all this trouble, I must have been overdoing it, is my bike damaged?' (keen cyclists are like this, bike first self last).

I replied 'These blokes are well trained, the ambulance is on its way and your bike is fine.'

The rangers spoke to him to keep him at ease. It takes a while for an ambulance to get up here and after half an hour the man began to show signs of distress. First aid checks were still being made and the rangers reassured him that he would be all right.

'I'm going, I can feel it, I'm not going to make it!'

'It's ok, try and relax, the ambulance will be here soon.' The ranger was doing his utmost.

'No I can feel it, everything's gone blurred, I can't see properly, I'm going.'

At this point one ranger was walking the verge ten or so yards away and shouted back 'Are these your glasses mate?'

The ambulance arrived and as he was being put aboard he shouted 'Me bike, me bike, what about me bike?'

'Don't worry,' I said. 'It'll be kept safe for you down at the cycle hire.'

A few weeks later his wife turned up at the centre to collect the bicycle. She reported him being well and back home.

'He sent you this bottle of whisky, he says thanks for all that you have done.'

I replied 'We'll say thank you to him on behalf of the others that did the first aid, it will get shared.'

'No!' she exclaimed. 'It's for you for looking after his bike, he was very concerned about it.'

I have been a shepherd up Derwent Valley now for sixteen years - the last seven of which have seen me installed at Ashes Farm as Tenant to the National Trust. Just short of one hundred acres of steep hillside keeps me busy all year round at weekends when I'm not hill shepherding at the larger farm next door. Hill farming is very close to nature as you follow the seasons as you work. Virtually all the work is outside so waterproof and warm boots and coats are a necessity in the winter months.

You can never tire of working with hill sheep and cattle. No two months do you do the same type of work. Winter feeding of the stock gives way to lambing, turning the sheep back onto the moors, gathering again to shear the ewes and dip the lambs, then calving the cows outside. As July approaches the hay making tackle is given a last servicing then it is all hands on deck once a good spell of weather appears - cutting and turning the hay until it is fit for the bales - and then nicely stacked in the barn before the rain can fall and spoil the crop.

Lambs are weaned in September then ewes are sorted and the older ones drafted to be sold. In November the tups are put to the ewes and the cycle begins again. Sounds idyllic? It can be, but adverse weather can hinder or ruin any of these operations. Good years rely on good weather. We are totally dependant on the climate in the hills - it dictates what you do and when you do it. Fog can ruin and stop a morning's sheep gathering and then lift and disappear within minutes of your return to the homestead. Wet weather can kill newborn lambs in minutes, sometimes can ruin hay crops, make steep fields impassable with a vehicle, while snow literally brings life an impassable with a vehicle, while snow literally brings life on the hill to a complete standstill - often with disastrous results.

Whoever decided to build a series of reservoirs in the upper Derwent Valley was a well-read and clever chap. Rainfall is one thing we have rather a lot of. This gives us less leeway than some other places. On dry days you do as much as possible because tomorrow can often return to rain. This is our way of farming - work with the weather as you have no other choice.

Another aspect we now have to work with is the increasing number of tourist to the area. Sheer numbers of visitors can make gathering sheep off the moor much more difficult as sheep tend to move away from people. Bringing a few hundred sheep down the dam sides takes more manpower now as we have to get the sheep past hoards of walkers. Luckily for us the vast amount of people do their utmost to keep out of the way by walking up the banks to let the sheep past. Some, however, insist on lying in the middle of the track, cameras snapping wildly as sheep veer off up the thick woodland - causing us a headache and our dogs more unnecessary work in getting the sheep back.

Most midweek visitors to the valley are lovely people who appreciate the countryside and want to be part of it. Weekenders, however, are often just families or friends out on leisure strolls.

Though I am sure no wilful damage is ever done the opening of gates, climbing of fences, knocking down walls are an almost daily occurrence somewhere up the valley.

My landlords have just had to spend a great deal of money to install a flagged footpath through a hay meadow to halt the erosion and damage caused by the increasing numbers of mountain bikes using the bridleway. Again I am sure that none of the users of the path would wilfully try to cause any damage at all, but it is the sheer numbers that accelerate any damage.

Derwent is a beautiful place - the number of people who visit each year is a testament to its beauty, and it is going to stay that way if things don't get any worse for the people of the countryside. The marvels of Derwent Valley are man-made - the Gothic dam walls, the water, the planted trees and the green fields are all due to man's hand. People should remember that man can make beautiful things and keep them beautiful. He does not have to destroy everything that he touches.

Up at the very top of the Derwent Reservoir just below the second dam wall there is a little patch of trees and a grassy track that leads down to the water. I ride up there a lot at the moment on my horse. When the sun is

Feeding Ewes in Winter

shining the water glistens and the air is as fresh as it could ever be. It's like a little patch of heaven. The dam wall stands majestically in front of me when I stop the horse and everything is perfect. There's no one there except a few Canada geese, may be the odd squirrel, no sounds but the water lapping against the bank and the birds singing in the trees. I get excited when I know I'm going to ride up here, because just for a few moments in an otherwise hectic day I have total peace.

You could say that my roots are well and truly in Derwent. My grandfather came here to work at Ashes farm in the mid 1930s and in 1943, aged 25 with a wife and three young daughters took the tenancy of Old House Farm, a National Trust owned farm which he farmed for 40 years and raised five daughters.

My mother, the second daughter was married in 1960 and moved into another local National Trust House - The Shooting Lodge, where I was born and grew up along with my brother and two sisters. We were real 'country kids', used to making our own entertainment which usually involved numerous animals, making dens, playing in streams, climbing trees, rope 'Tarzan' swings and riding old tattered bicycles.

I was always interested in farming, particularly sheep and dogs, which wasn't really surprising as we lived in the middle of the farm and my grandad loved to share his knowledge of the countryside. School holidays and weekends were mostly spent up at the farm, helping with the lambing or shearing, so when I left school I decided to go to agricultural college, and I've been shepherding ever since.

In family tradition I am a tenant of the 'National Trust' which I suppose is inevitable as the Trust own much of the land and houses in the Derwent Valley.

I must say that if my house was on the open market I couldn't possibly afford to buy or rent it, or any other houses in the Derwent Valley, as hill farming wages can't possibly compete with professional salaries from nearby Sheffield and Manchester.

High House

I've been working in the Derwent Valley for the past seven years and it's certainly an eye opening experience. A great many of the incidents that have happened since I have been here are worth sharing, but only a select few can be printed.

I remember back in July 1995, a warm Wednesday afternoon, I was busy dealing with returning customers when a man turned up at the door.

'Excuse me, I need to see a ranger, it's very important, could you find me one?'

'No chance,' someone replied, 'Haven't seen one all day, but I will try and find one with the radio.' No replies came after many transmissions.

'Sorry no rangers, can we help?'

'Well, I've got a bomb in my car!'

'Er, you've got a bomb?'

'Yes, we were coming off Howden Edge and I found a bomb in a dried up stream, so I carried it down, put it in the car and drove down here."

'So what do you suggest?' I asked, I had already decided he was stupid.

'Well, er, can I leave it here?'

'It looks like you will have to, do you realise that you have done a very stupid thing and that you are putting a lot of people in serious danger?' He didn't reply so I carried on. 'Take me to your car and let me see it.'

So we arrived at his car where we found his wife, she was very agitated and immediately began an argument with her husband telling him he should have left it where it was and marked the spot instead of bringing it all the way down with them. Meanwhile I was viewing the device with a good deal of caution. I did try to explain that it could be a practice shell and that my colleague was arranging for the bomb disposal unit to come out. However, the arguing between man and wife was too loud and it was attracting a crowd of people all wanting to know what was going on. When the man eventually stopped to draw enough breath to explain to the crowd that he had a bomb in his car, I witnessed the fastest car park clearance I've ever seen.

'Right!' I said at last, 'Take it up there into the trees and mark it with something so the bomb disposal men can find it.'

'What me? You are joking, I'm not carrying it,' he retorted.

So now I was rude, VERY RUDE!! I pointed out that he had carried it a least three miles and driven nearly five with it, so it wouldn't make a deal of difference and as an adult it was his responsibility. With this he put the bomb down on the floor, got into his car and drove away.

It was put into a safe place. I waited until 9pm and kept contacting bomb disposal head quarters. They arrived at 10am the next day to inform us that thank heavens it was a harmless remnant. It seems that there are people who come into the countryside and cannot be responsible for their own actions and expect that someone else will sort out the situations that they create for themselves but cannot handle.

Grandad, a sheep farmer, was moving some sheep from the steep field behind our house, working his dogs whilst driving his Landrover. He got out of the Landrover to close the gate after the sheep, and as soon as his back was turned, it started to roll down the field. It went hurtling down the field, veered to the right and straight into the stone field wall, where it came to a sudden stop. We all ran out in a panic on hearing the crash, to see Grandad walking down the field.

'Oh well, never mind' said Grandad casually, it's making the gap up in the wall.' He let his dog out of the back and walked home, leaving us all speechless.

I was up on Howden moors in my ex-army Jeep with a friend. I had been in the same place a couple of weeks earlier with my father-in-law who farmed the moors, and we had come down off the moor on a steep track. I 'found' this track and started to drive down. After a short while I thought to myself 'I don't remember it being as steep as this!' The track curved around the hillside, and as the jeep got to the bottom it met up with a stone wall across the track. I realised that I was obviously on the wrong track completely, this one being a disused sledge track from bygone days. The track was so steep that the jeep would not reverse up. We walked home and fetched snow-chains for the wheels and a block and tackle to winch the jeep out. Nothing we did could move the jeep, so we ended up taking the wall down, driving the jeep through the gap and into the woods, rebuilding the wall, and then having to fell two trees in order to drive down the woods and back onto the road below.

The fields at Ashes Farm are very steep, so hay-making there is still quite traditional and labour intensive. The whole family is roped in to lend a hand, and as nobody is left to mind the children, they often play in the fields nearby where a close eye can be kept on their safety.

Exposure to the sun is a constant worry, so everybody is smothered in sun block and wears wide-brimmed hats.

One day my sister noted with frustration that her three year old had once again discarded his hat despite numerous warnings of the dangers of exposure to the sun.

'Tom,' she cried, 'Where's your hat? Put it on!'

'I don't need a hat,' he reassured her 'I want the sun to stroke my head.'

I walk this track around 7.30 in an evening, it is so peaceful then with only the flora and fauna, and a handful of fishermen to disturb me and my dogs. The smell of fresh grass, bracken, sheep and lots of fresh air is my companion. The sounds are of sheep and lambs, of ducks and Canada geese also fisherman casting their lines. The noise of planes taking off and landing over the hill and of course cars going up and down the Derwent Road hitting the cattle grids.

I love the late Spring for colours and Autumn as the trees take on such different hues.

The high hills surround me and tall trees, grassy banks and of course water. Luckily there aren't many people around then so my two dogs,

Wellhead Barn

(Labrador and Jack Russell) have a free reign and race off for a swim while I sit on one of the seats erected in memory of people who loved the valley.

The one I always sit on is in memory of Peter the man who started the Ladybower Fishing Club.

What a wonderful place.

This is a real, early in the morning - just as the day is dawning, Postman Pat kind of delivery. I have been a postman for forty-five years, the last three years in the Valley. The Derwent Valley must be one of the most picturesque deliveries in the country. The Valley is at it's most beautiful when the sun is shining on it. Although it does have it's angry side, that is when it is covered in ice and snow, it can be positively dangerous. The milk lady and the postman always try to get through, though. Like Postman Pat I have made many friends around the valley. Come along with me and meet some of them.

Ian Butler: Dale End Cottage. Ian has been a good friend and helped me a lot. I have an allotment in Sheffield (where I live) I don't have a greenhouse though, Ian does. He also has a propagator and knows how to use it. Ian has started off, many dozens of cabbage, cauliflower, leeks, and sweetpeas for me. All I have to do with God's help, is watch them grow. In return I supply some fresh veg! I get a real bargain.

Stan Hitch: Ashopton Woodyard. Stan always has a word. He could also have a 'wad' of leaflets for me to deliver. These leaflets are concerning social events and council news for residents around the Valleys. The leaflets are in fact from Stan's wife Dorothy, who is a Councillor.

My reward for this favour, is a bottle of brandy and a hug and a kiss from Dorothy, at Christmas.

Eric Elliot: Ding Bank Farm. Eric always comes out to meet me. He collects his mail and Yorkshire Post. Eric is a real interesting character. We will have a chat. I know more about - 'Doggin' now that Eric has explained it all too me. Look out for the dogs!! There could be five or six very expensive dogs running round the van.

Peter Wood: Crook Hill Farm. At Crookhill, situated high on the hillside, over looking the Ladybower reservoir, I always get a warm welcome - good chat and a lot of leg pulling. Peter Wood still thinks my job is a lot easier than farming - well I ask you. Janet sometimes gives me home-made oatcakes, they are delicious. Watch the dog - Rocky - he does not like Postmen; once bitten, I'm now twice shy.

We now travel a good two miles, with the Ladybower on our right, past the Derwent Dam wall and along to Birchenlee. Then on we go to the Howden Dam, where we deliver Beavers Croft. We now come all the way back and go to the other side of the valley.

Derwent Lodge. This is one address where I loved to call. I looked forward to my chat with Tom Salt. Tom could tell a good tale. I love a good story. I would take Tom his newspaper every day and collect his lottery ticket every Friday. Tom, solemnly promised me, one million pounds sterling if ever he won the jackpot. I could have talked to Tom for hours, if only I had the time. It was a sad day for me, when Tom died.

Jubilee Cottage. Amy Ollerenshaw, who has sadly died, was another good friend of mine. Amy, who was eighty-six when she died, would always have a cup of tea ready for me. She would have a roaring fire in the winter. I would call every day with a newspaper. Luckily, I was on hand, to call the doctor the day Amy was taken poorly. We could gossip, me and Amy.

Now, its way on down the back of the valley. We could see more people who I consider friends, Peter Fryer, Mick Jolley, Kath Birkinshaw, Samantha Wood and her daughter Jo Jo.

It's now time for our meal break, today it is fine and warm so we will literally drive down to the Ladybower. This is a secret place, where I can almost put the front wheels of the van in to the water and park in the shade of a cherry tree. I switch the engine off and listen to the wild life. Some of the wild birds recognise the van by now. Chaffinch, blue tits, mallards with their young all come to share my sandwiches. After breakfast, we travel back to the A57 Snake Pass to continue the delivery. Now that's another story.

My favourite place is the Snake Summit on the A57. As this is a busy main road few travellers stop to look around being too busy to reach their destination. But from here you have a completely clear view (on a good day) in every direction, to the north Bleaklow Hill, to the East and Northeast the Moors stretch out to Derwent Edge with the upper Alport and Derwent Valleys within modest walking distance. To the West looking out over Manchester, Ashton-Under-Lyne to Oldham and Southwest on a very good day the river Mersey can be seen.

The Moor is special - early evening in late Spring, after a sunny day when the warmth is still in the air and the smell of grass and moist earth rises. There are hares in the field on the hill bordering the Moor - brown Mountain - large and yet fragile, and rabbits - smaller and more compact. You can hear the hum of bees in the sycamores and the sound of birds - first swallows scouting for nesting sites and pursuing early insects - small birds calling for mates or warning of a tawny owl. Further away the sound of the Mill Brook and curlew - lonely and yet familiar. Around you are the sheep and the occasional pheasant. Lambs sound lost and insolvent but reassuring. Flowers are small and unobtrusive yet part of the essential pattern . To top it all are the sky views - brilliant sunset or clear with an early moon.

My favourite place is Barrow Stones, high on the moors, early in the afternoon, with the smells of heather and bracken and noises from the wildlife, grouse, skylark and meadow pippit.
Colours are dark brown, purple and there are sandy tracks to lay and rest and absorb the fantastic atmosphere, the dark brown and purple colours,the weather beaten rocks on the skyline, to try and be at one with the landscape.

The Upper Derwent Valley

Mill Brook is not far from here but it is some times very loud because people are having lunch or some food or children are playing in the water and shouting and screaming. Some times there is just you so you can go over the stones; go off jumps and up hills. When the water is up you can go up to the car park because there are piles of stone to go over. Most of the time I go down to Millbrook with my friend Andrew.

The school taxi drops me off at the bottom of the ramp and I get prepared for the long trek up the steep, stoney, usually muddy track. The first part is the most tiresome - it's the steepest. Up and over the first cattle grid. By this time I've usually started singing a song. In the field I can see rabbits scuttling into their burrows. I look down and see the farmer hanging out his washing accompanied by the yapping of his dogs.

Past the wall and ahead of me, I can see yet another cattle grid. The view down the valley now opens and I see the trees' reflections on the reservoir but as I go across the cattle grid the wall blocks my view.

Ahead of me I see mountain hares bounding across the field. As I walk past Bullhead there are a variety of animals; wood pigeons clattering out of the trees, pheasants shepherding their young and occasionally you might get a glimpse of a stoat or weasel. By this time without knowing it I am already at the third and final cattle grid, across it and I now am in the field with the sheep. I chase them off the track by imitating a dog (sometimes successful, sometimes not).Through the final gate and at last what a relief. I can see home. I run along the last few metres and open the yard gate, pat Matt and Meg (our two sheepdogs), walk past the car and enter the house through the barn, dump my bags on the floor and at last I'M HOME!

Walking home from school